LIGHTNING MCQUEEN

Racing legend Lightning McQueen has inspired fans around the world. The seven-time winner of the Piston Cup has earned his place as one of the greats. His speed and passion make him unstoppable!

Team Lightning

Lightning loves to hang out with his buddies from his hometown, Radiator Springs. The support of Sally, Mater and other pals gives him the strength to succeed!

Rust-eze logo

Winning smile

Friendly competition

Racers can be friends as well as rivals. Lightning respects his fellow trackmates and often shares a joke with them after a race.

> "Okay, here we go. Focus. Speed. I am speed."
>
> Lightning McQueen

Focused and friendly

Lightning's hard work has made him a champion. However, off the track he is laid-back, loyal and friendly. His wheels are firmly on the ground!

8

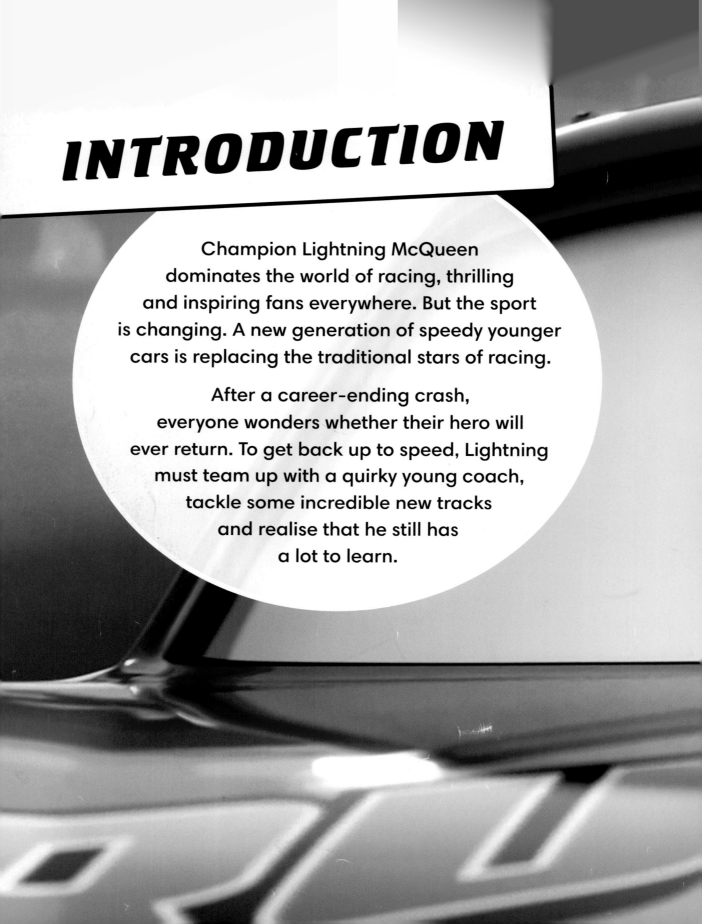

INTRODUCTION

Champion Lightning McQueen
dominates the world of racing, thrilling
and inspiring fans everywhere. But the sport
is changing. A new generation of speedy younger
cars is replacing the traditional stars of racing.

After a career-ending crash,
everyone wonders whether their hero will
ever return. To get back up to speed, Lightning
must team up with a quirky young coach,
tackle some incredible new tracks
and realise that he still has
a lot to learn.

True or False?

Lightning McQueen used to be part of Team Dinoco.

FALSE: He has been sponsored by Rust-eze, makers of medicated bumper ointment, since day one.

Storm warning

Lightning McQueen is surprised by the success of rookie racer Jackson Storm. When the brash newbie starts to get results, McQueen realises he has a serious rival.

McQueen's custom red paintwork

LIGHTNING MCQUEEN

TOP SPEED:	198 mph/318 kph
START TIME:	0-60 in 4 seconds
VEHICLE TYPE:	2006 Custom-built Piston Cup Racer
ENGINE:	Full Race V-8 with 750 hp

INSIDE MCQUEEN!

What makes a champion like Lightning McQueen? Here's a chance to look under the sheet metal and find out exactly what a winner is made of.

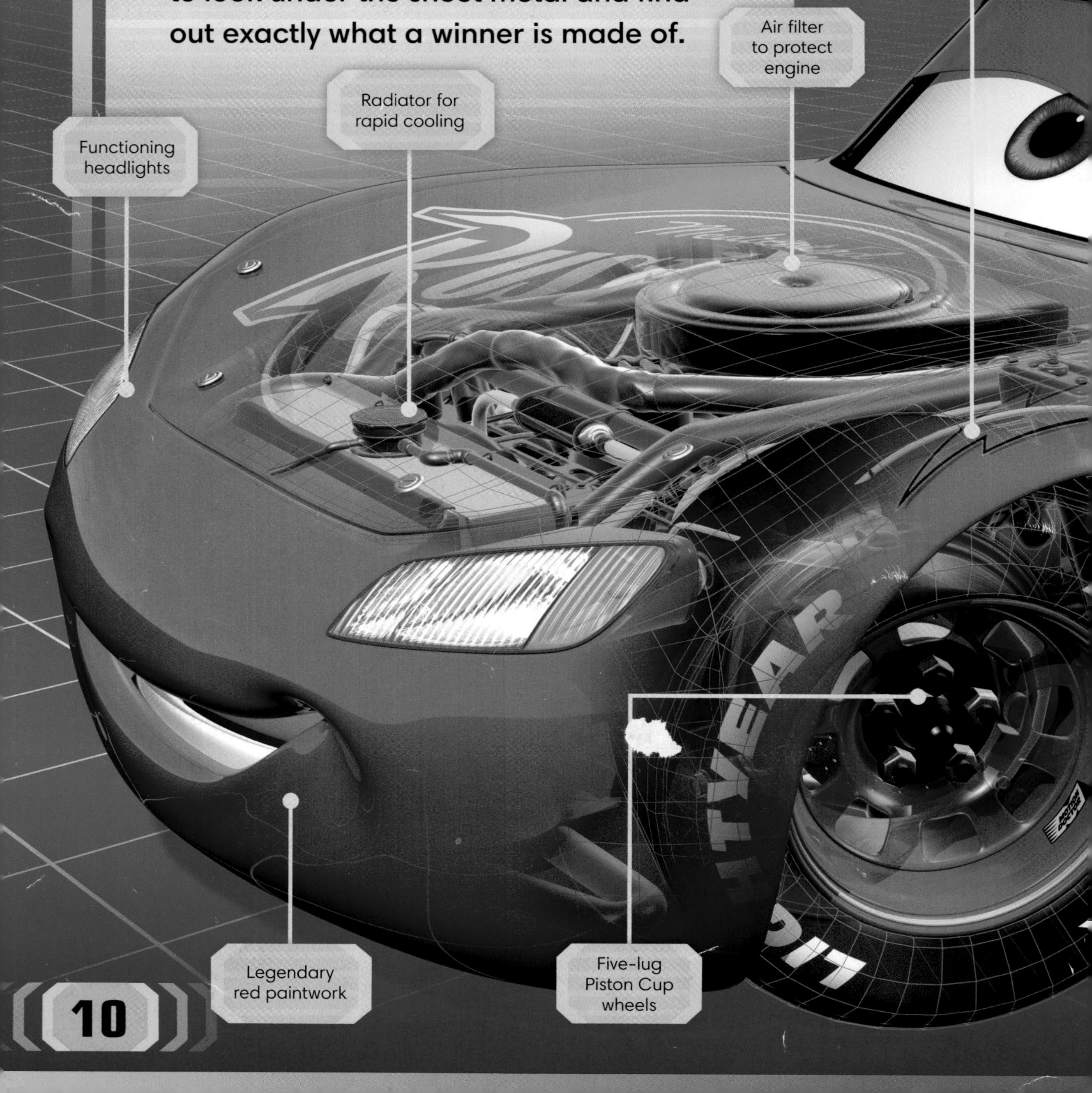

Lucky lightning bolt

Air filter to protect engine

Radiator for rapid cooling

Functioning headlights

Legendary red paintwork

Five-lug Piston Cup wheels

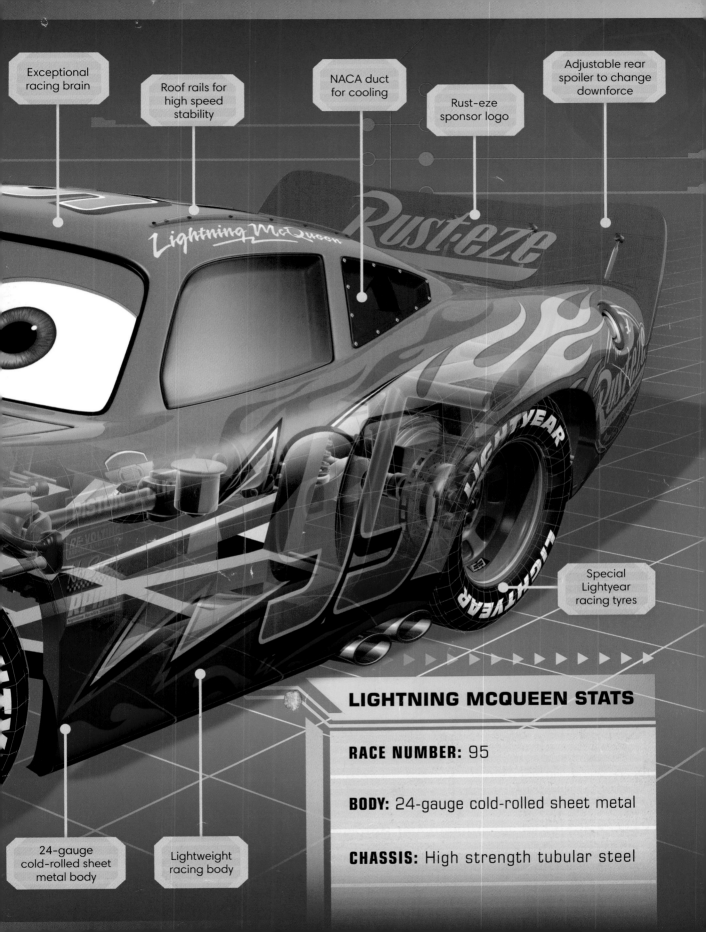

Exceptional racing brain

Roof rails for high speed stability

NACA duct for cooling

Rust-eze sponsor logo

Adjustable rear spoiler to change downforce

Special Lightyear racing tyres

24-gauge cold-rolled sheet metal body

Lightweight racing body

LIGHTNING MCQUEEN STATS

RACE NUMBER: 95

BODY: 24-gauge cold-rolled sheet metal

CHASSIS: High strength tubular steel

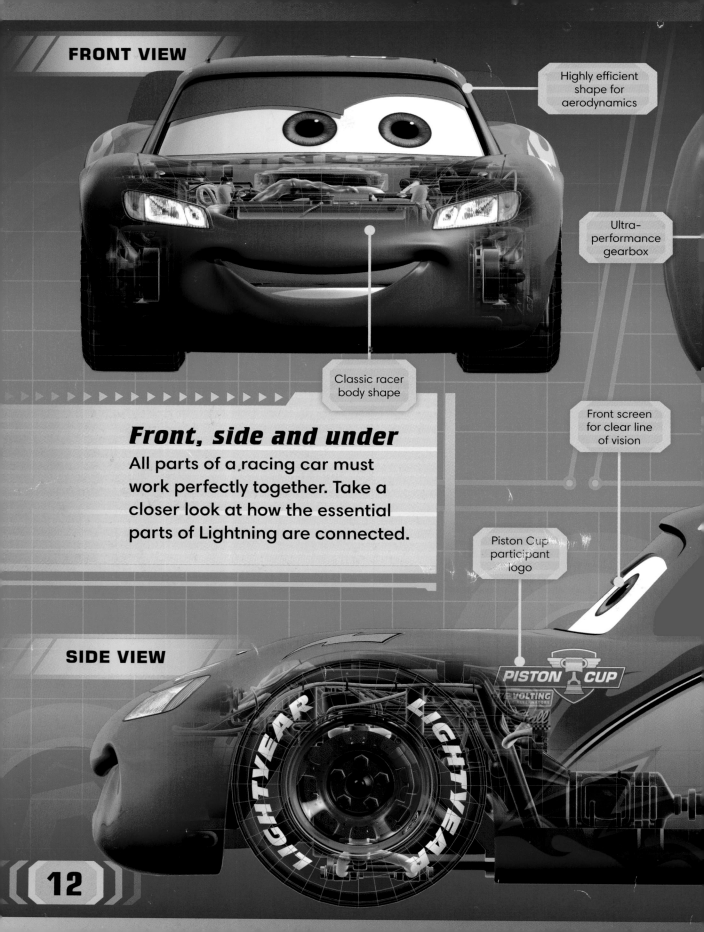

FRONT VIEW

Highly efficient shape for aerodynamics

Ultra-performance gearbox

Front screen for clear line of vision

Classic racer body shape

Front, side and under

All parts of a racing car must work perfectly together. Take a closer look at how the essential parts of Lightning are connected.

Piston Cup participant logo

SIDE VIEW

PISTON CUP

UNDER VIEW

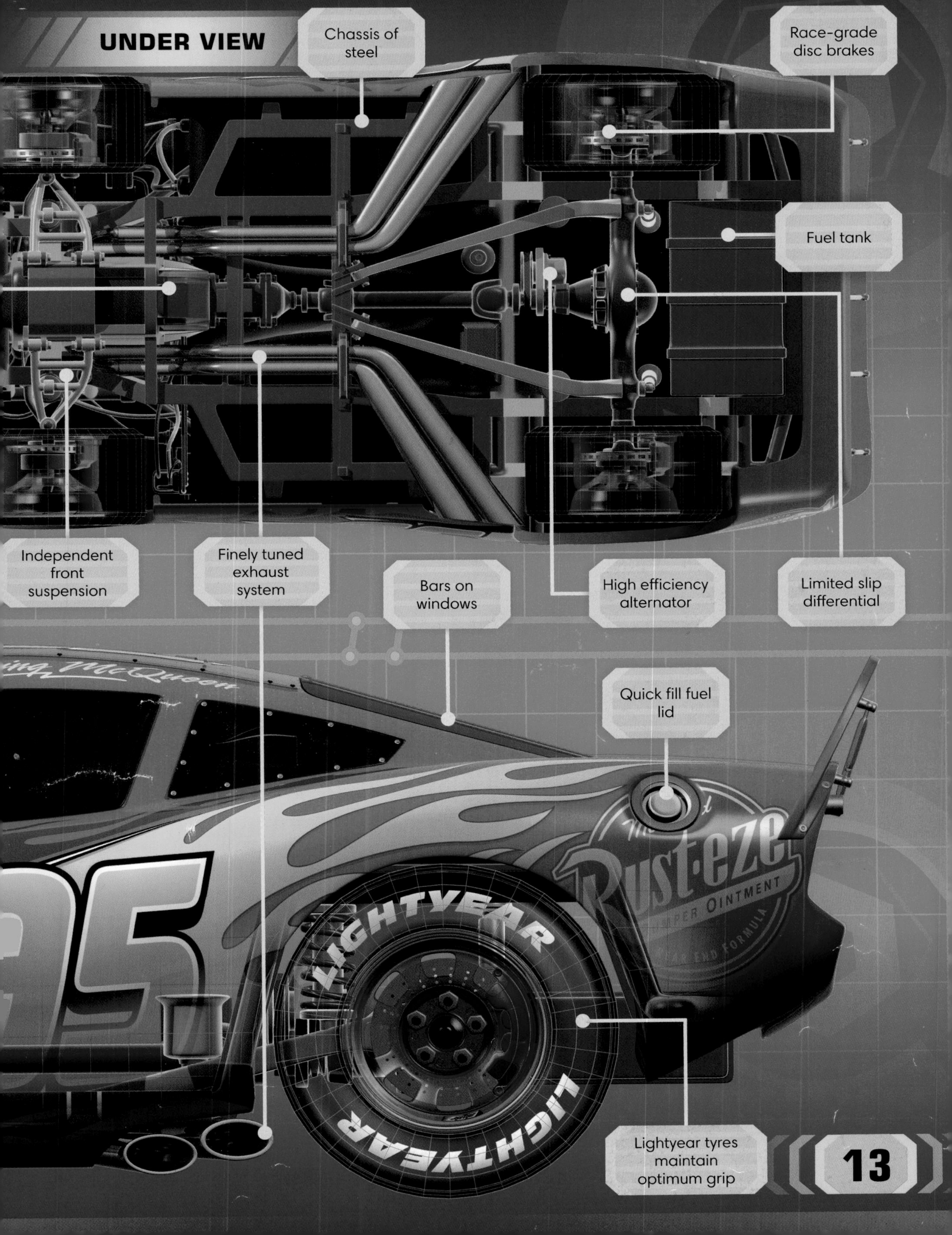

Chassis of steel
Race-grade disc brakes
Fuel tank
Independent front suspension
Finely tuned exhaust system
Bars on windows
High efficiency alternator
Limited slip differential
Quick fill fuel lid
Rust-eze
OINTMENT
LIGHTYEAR
LIGHTYEAR
Lightyear tyres maintain optimum grip

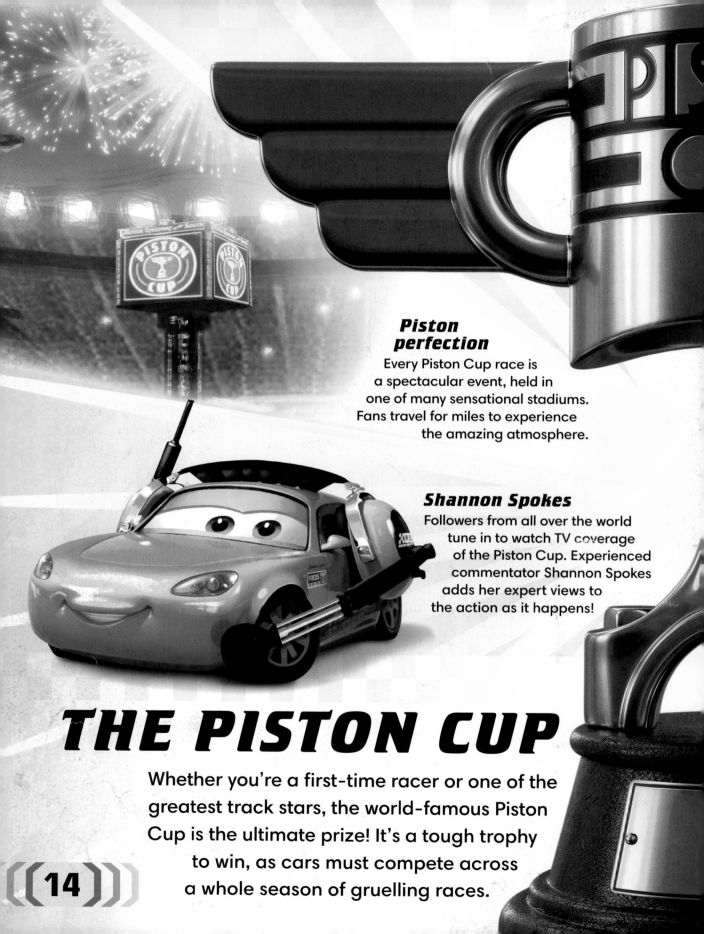

Piston perfection

Every Piston Cup race is a spectacular event, held in one of many sensational stadiums. Fans travel for miles to experience the amazing atmosphere.

Shannon Spokes

Followers from all over the world tune in to watch TV coverage of the Piston Cup. Experienced commentator Shannon Spokes adds her expert views to the action as it happens!

THE PISTON CUP

Whether you're a first-time racer or one of the greatest track stars, the world-famous Piston Cup is the ultimate prize! It's a tough trophy to win, as cars must compete across a whole season of gruelling races.

Race risks

With the crowded track and ultra-high speeds, racing in the Piston Cup is dangerous. Serious injuries are rare, but even experienced racers must be careful.

Press and paparazzi

Every race is covered by journalists desperate to get an exclusive interview or photo of the winner! They report on all the latest developments, feeding fans with every detail on the Piston Cup!

Gale Beaufort

As Jackson Storm's high-tech transporter, Gale Beaufort makes sure she is colour-coordinated and just as sleek. With her slick exterior, Gale looks like a force to be reckoned with!

Storming ahead

Storm is all about speed and power, but does he have the real-life race experience to beat Lightning to the Piston Cup?

Aerodynamics designed for speed

"You have no idea what a pleasure it is to finally beat you."

Jackson Storm

Rude racer

Storm may be talented, but he has a lot to learn about treating others with respect. The overconfident contender is also obsessed with being in the spotlight.

JACKSON STORM

Jackson Storm has shaken up the world of racing! This ambitious Next Gen is streamlined for speed. He is confident that nothing will stop him from winning the Piston Cup – not even Lightning McQueen.

Simulator success

Storm trains on a high-tech race simulator instead of on an actual track. He believes that using virtual reality to analyse his performance gives him the edge.

Confident expression

JACKSON STORM

TOP SPEED:	214 mph/345 kph
START TIME:	0-60 in 3.6 seconds
VEHICLE TYPE:	2017 Custom-built Next Gen Piston Cup Racer
ENGINE:	Maximum Performance V-8 with 850 hp

State-of-the-art tyres

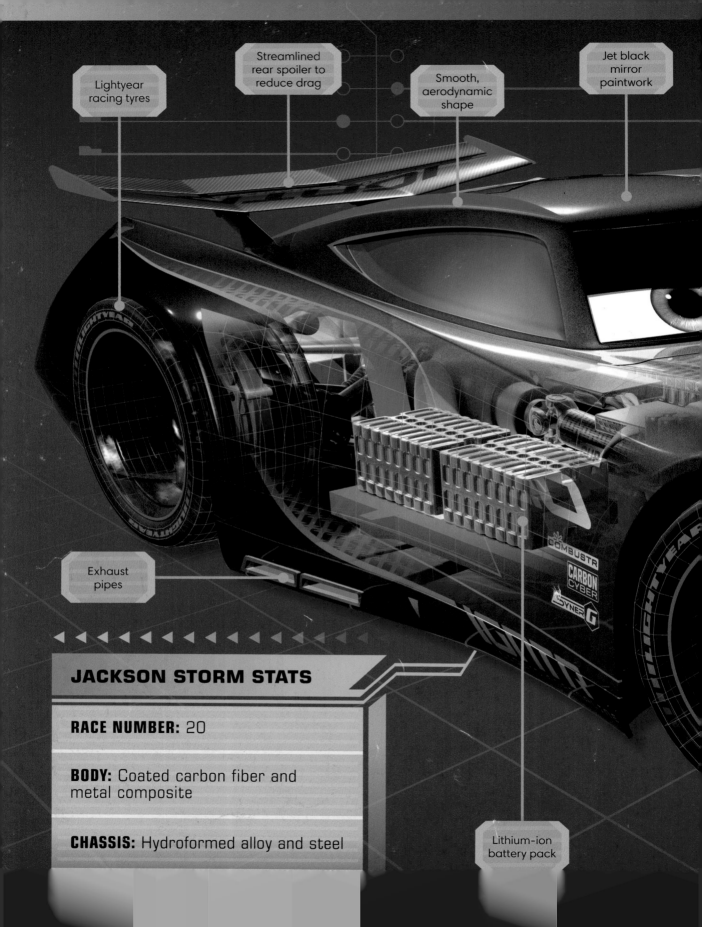

Lightyear racing tyres

Streamlined rear spoiler to reduce drag

Smooth, aerodynamic shape

Jet black mirror paintwork

Exhaust pipes

COMBUSTR

CARBON CYBER

SYNER G

JACKSON STORM STATS

RACE NUMBER: 20

BODY: Coated carbon fiber and metal composite

CHASSIS: Hydroformed alloy and steel

Lithium-ion battery pack

INSIDE STORM!

Jackson Storm is always focused on speed – both in the way he is built and the way he thinks. Take a tour around the vehicle everyone's talking about!

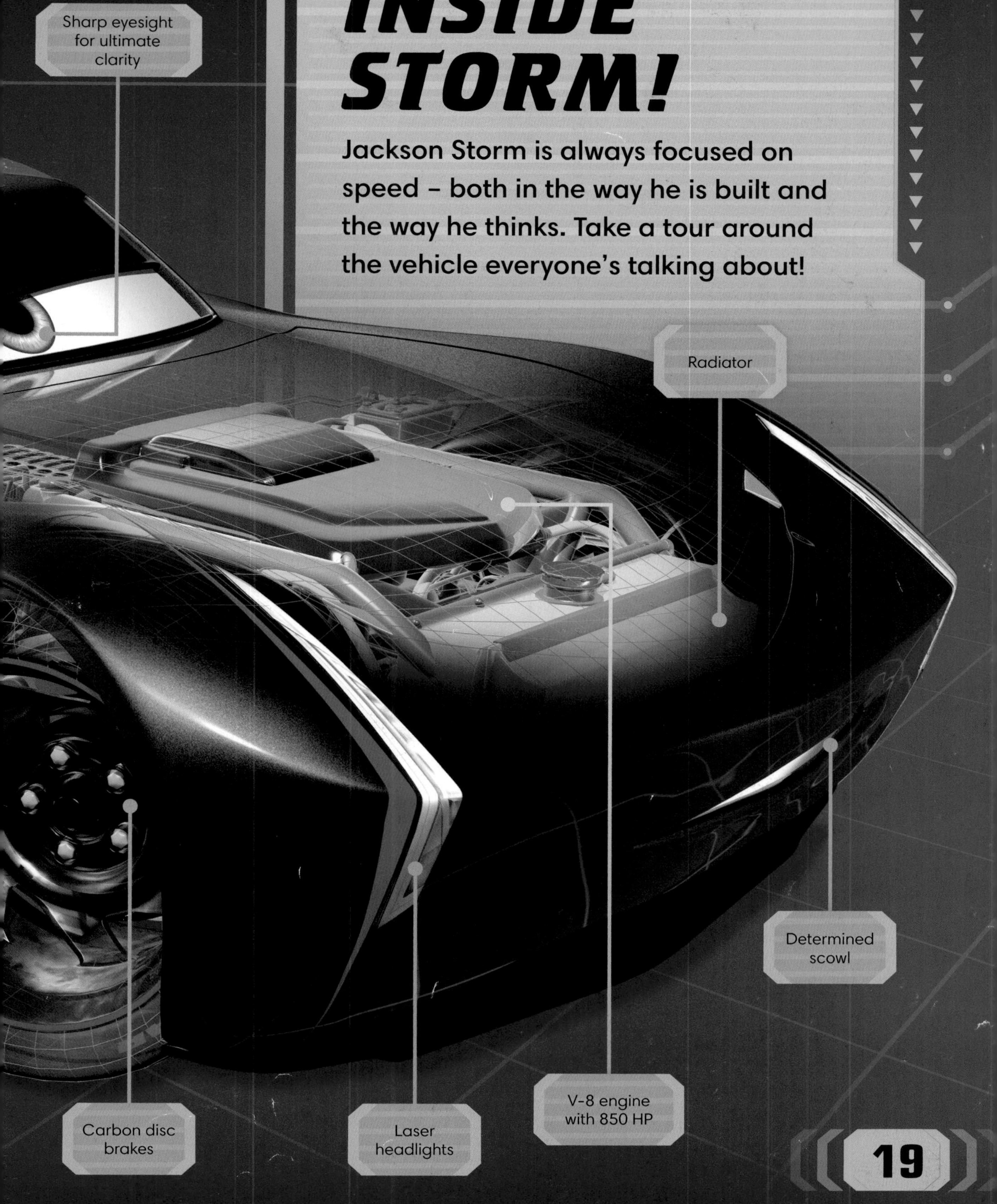

Sharp eyesight for ultimate clarity

Radiator

Determined scowl

Carbon disc brakes

Laser headlights

V-8 engine with 850 HP

19

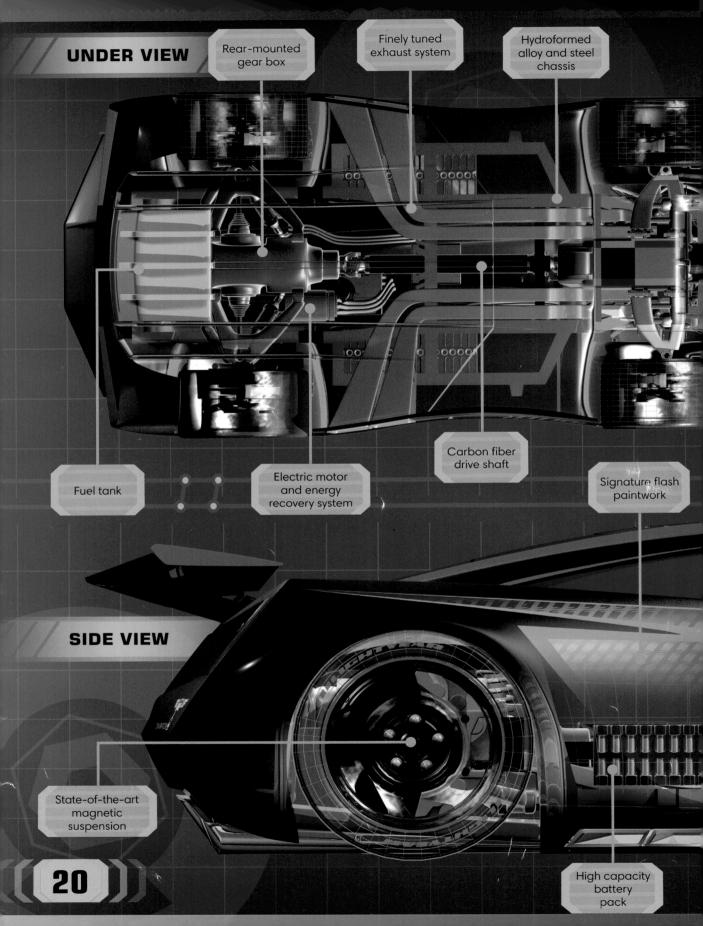

UNDER VIEW

Rear-mounted gear box

Finely tuned exhaust system

Hydroformed alloy and steel chassis

Fuel tank

Electric motor and energy recovery system

Carbon fiber drive shaft

Signature flash paintwork

SIDE VIEW

State-of-the-art magnetic suspension

High capacity battery pack

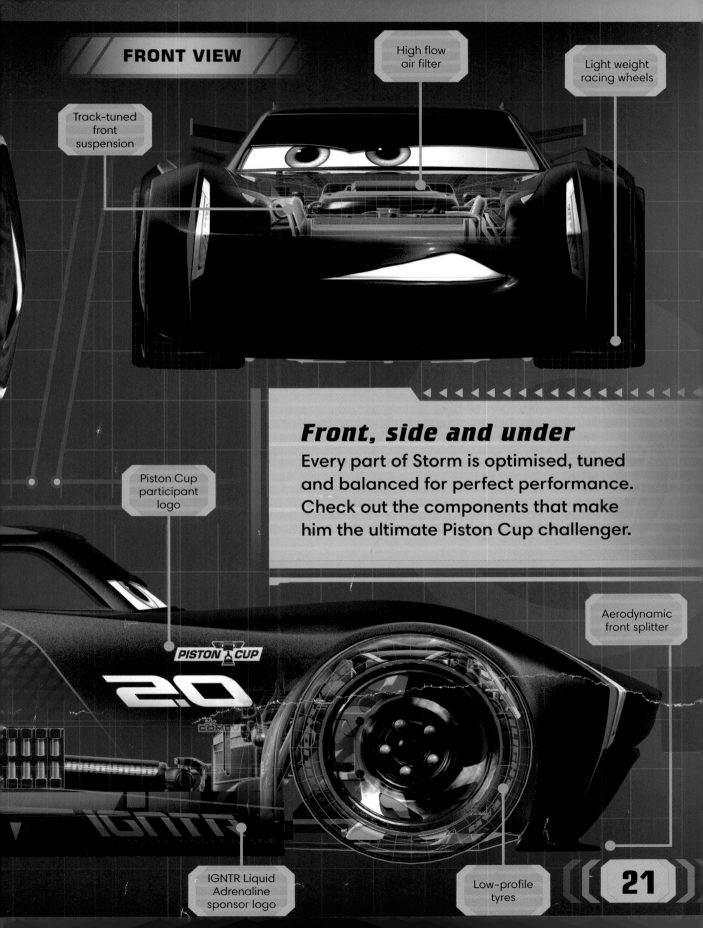

High flow air filter

Light weight racing wheels

Track-tuned front suspension

Front, side and under

Every part of Storm is optimised, tuned and balanced for perfect performance. Check out the components that make him the ultimate Piston Cup challenger.

Piston Cup participant logo

PISTON CUP

20

IGNTR

Aerodynamic front splitter

IGNTR Liquid Adrenaline sponsor logo

Low-profile tyres

High tech

Next Gens use the latest technology to improve their performance. Full motion platform simulators and wind tunnels help increase their speed. Everyone is shocked by the results!

A new era

At first, Lightning McQueen and his racing pals don't worry too much about the the Next Gens. But when the young rookies start producing impressive results, they realise that the sport is changing.

THE NEXT GENERATION

Next-generation racers are high tech, high speed and highly successful! A new wave of young, modern Next Gens are ripping up the racing rule book, and are rapidly replacing the old-school competitors.

Have you heard?

One of Lightning's racing pals, Bobby Swift, is replaced Gen on the actual day of a Piston Cup race!

Next Gen numbers

Racing pundit Natalie Certain charts the Next Gens' success by using her analytics and data. Natalie's TV reports explain how they do so much better than the traditional racers.

Old-school racer: Brick Yardley

Next-gen racer: Chase Racelott

Last one standing

There's no bigger rivalry between a traditional and a next-gen racer than that between Lightning McQueen and Jackson Storm. McQueen is eventually the only one of the old guard left competing.

The race to retire

Race sponsors are dropping old-school racers in favour of the new cars, forcing many of Lightning's friends to retire. Next Gens are taking the colours and numbers of the cars that they replaced.

NATALIE CERTAIN

TV racing pundit Natalie Certain believes that there's nothing greater than data. The analyst uses her mathematical mind to predict the winner of each race. Many viewers count on her predictions!

Lightning to lose?

Natalie's statistics tell her that Jackson Storm is "96.8% unstoppable" to win and beat Lightning McQueen. Is she wrong to write Lightning off so easily?

Number cruncher

Natalie is certain that data is always right. However, her calculations don't take into account the incredible passion that drives champions like Lightning McQueen!

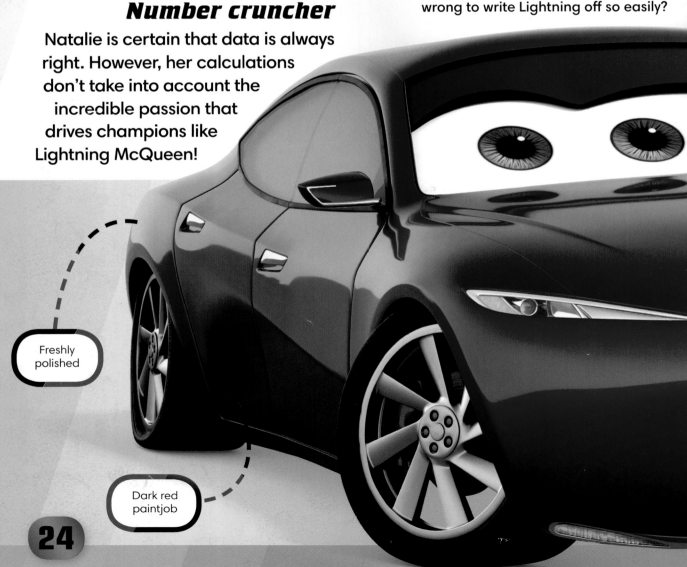

Freshly polished

Dark red paintjob

Bitter Chick

Natalie appears on a TV show named *Chick's Picks*. It is presented by Chick Hicks, an old racing rival of Lightning McQueen. These days, the vile veteran uses his show to fire cheap insults at his former nemesis!

Amazing analytical mind

Fact-packed!

Natalie's knowledge of racers is amazing! She's an expert on everything from weight distribution to aerodynamics.

NATALIE CERTAIN

OCCUPATION:	Statistical analyst
TOP SPEED:	27 calculations per minute
SPECIALTY:	Near-genius number crunching
VEHICLE TYPE:	Evolv Motors Provoc Quantus 4S

"The racing world is changing." Natalie Certain

NUMBERS DON'T LIE

So you want to be a racing data analyst? The first thing you need to learn is that the numbers don't lie! There's a huge amount of racer data to help predict a winner. Here's my lowdown on the downforce, optimum speed and some of the other key factors you'll need. Good luck!

Have you heard?

Natalie has correctly predicted more Piston Cup winners than any other race pundit.

WEIGHT DISTRIBUTION

The weight distribution of a car is the amount of weight in the front compared to the back. This can seriously affect the speed of the car, so every racer needs to find their ideal balance.

CONSISTENCY

A consistent racer is a winning racer. A car who can hold their position on every single lap of a race is more likely to take top spot on the podium.

OPTIMUM SPEED

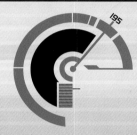

It's not always about top speed, but the speed a car can hold lap after lap. If it's higher than their rival racers, then you know that's the winner!

DRAG COEFFICIENT

The aerodynamics of a car — how its shape meets the oncoming air — heavily affects performance. The lower the "drag coefficient" number, the less the car is slowed down from oncoming air.

TYRE PRESSURE

The amount of air in a racer's tyres must be optimised for speed, grip and safety. Tyre pressure levels are closely linked to each car's performance data.

DOWNFORCE

This is a downwards force produced by cars as they drive on the track. High downforce means that the racers increase the grip on the tyres as they go round corners.

THE FINAL RACE
★★ STORM TO SEAL THE DEAL ★★

Racing sensation Jackson Storm is expected to be the Piston Cup champion after today's final race of the season. With an incredible ten wins, this rookie has dominated the sport in his debut season!

PISTON 🏆 TIMES
RACING CHAMP CRASHES!

Lightning McQueen has been involved in a serious crash! The popular racer took a lot of damage when he lost control trying to overtake Jackson Storm. After receiving treatment, McQueen is set to return to Radiator Springs for a long recovery.

MCQUEEN THE HAS-BEEN?

Piston Cup fans wonder if the next race might be Lightning McQueen's last? McQueen has been unable to match Jackson Storm's performance. Many of his old trackmates have retired and been replaced by next-gen racers.

A FALLEN HERO

Is this the end for Lightning McQueen? No announcement has been made about his future. Statistical analyst Natalie Certain feels that McQueen's future is very uncertain. TV show host and former racer Chick Hicks seems happy to report that his old rival is down for the count.

Go, Lightning!

When Lightning decides to return to racing, his Radiator Springs pals give him a great send-off to the Racing Centre. They just know that he'll get back on top.

Banners in Lightning's colours

Corridors leading to many training rooms

Super Centre

From the practice track and grand waterway on the grounds, to the simulators in the jaw-dropping main building, the Rust-eze Centre has everything racers need. There's even a zen room!

Grand entrance hall

RUST-EZE RACING CENTRE

The brand new Rust-eze Racing Centre is the ultimate place for training racers. Packed full of the best equipment, the centre is geared toward producing the next generation of champions.

Huge number 95 sculpture

Sterling

The new Rust-eze owner, Sterling, has invested in creating the new centre. This business car's commitment to racing (and money-making) has delivered a world-class facility.

Rusty and Dusty

Racing legend

Lightning McQueen has long been with Rust-eze. The Racing Centre celebrates his legendary success with a collection of memorabilia and a huge number 95 to inspire other racers.

CRUZ RAMIREZ

Cruz Ramirez is a major factor in the success of the Next Gens. With her quirky coaching methods and instinct for knowing what makes a racer tick, Cruz can turn a rookie into a winner!

Sterling boss

Cruz's boss, Sterling, knows that she is an important part of the business. She makes racers go faster – which makes him more money.

"Ready to meet it, greet it, and defeat it?"
Cruz Ramirez

Bright yellow paintjob

Each of Cruz's tyres has a name!

True or False?

Cruz can go even faster than some of the racers she trains.

TRUE: She whizzes around the simulator track!

Top trainer

Cruz is the best trainer at the Rust-eze Racing Centre – and probably in the country! Her results are incredible, especially for someone so new to the business. She finds the best in each of her racers.

Ramirez the racer?

Cruz once dreamed of becoming a racer herself. She may enjoy training others, but deep down she still longs to be on the track.

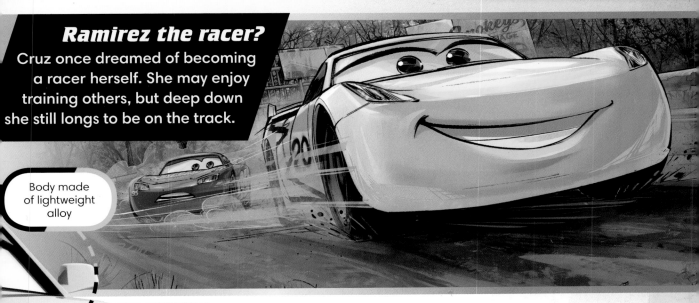

Body made of lightweight alloy

Full of fun

Training with Cruz is never dull! Her offbeat sense of humour, lively personality and unusual training methods means that there's often a surprise just around the corner!

CRUZ RAMIREZ

TOP SPEED:	210 mph/338 kph
START TIME:	0-60 in 3.8 seconds
VEHICLE TYPE:	2017 CRS Sports Coupe
ENGINE:	High performance DOHC V-6

Racing mind

When Mr. McQueen first saw me on the simulator, he mistook me for a racer. Perhaps it is because of my amazing lap times. I know that feeling in my engine of wanting to win!

Next-gen school

I've trained some of the best rookies that are aiming to qualify for the Piston Cup. They are young, hungry and eager to learn!

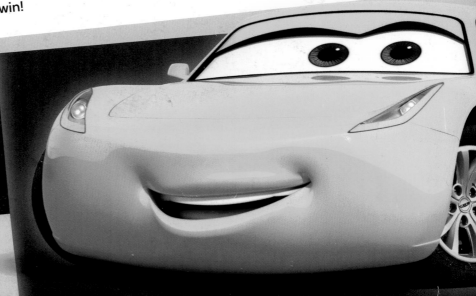

True or False?

As an example to the racers she trains, Cruz has a name for each of her wheels.

TRUE: They are named Maria, Juanita, Ronaldo and Debbie Richardson!

"It's all about motivation." Cruz Ramirez

Senior project

Mr. McQueen has a traditional approach. He isn't used to technology like the simulator and he's a little flabby around the tyres. I call him my senior project!

Time to train

I've set Mr. McQueen an intense training program. He does dance class and aerobics, and practices visualising beating Jackson Storm to get him in the zone.

CRUZ THE COACH

As a top trainer, I create the perfect program for each racer. I work on sharpening technical skills, get the guys in shape and focus on drive and ambition. Some even call me the Maestro of Motivation!

Have you heard?

Cruz uses music and pictures to help her racers focus, especially if they are feeling homesick.

"THE GREEN FLAG IS OUT."

THE RACING SIMULATOR

The simulator is the ultimate training device. Racers use a platform and screen to whizz round a virtual track. The simulator alerts racers with warnings whenever they make a mistake, no matter how big or small.

"YOU HAVE JUMPED A BARRIER."

"YOU HAVE DESTROYED A BUILDING."

"YOU ARE ON FIRE."

"DANGER. DANGER."

"YOU ARE GOING THE WRONG WAY."

"YOU HAVE HIT A WALL."

"YOU HAVE CRASHED. YOU HAVE CRASHED."

Practice makes perfect

By notching up the difficulty of the racing conditions on the simulator, you can learn how to be – and how to beat – the very best!

Stormy skies

Abandoned pier

Stays on the hardpacked sand.

Lightning speeding ahead

FIREBALL BEACH

Racers love to practice at the old Fireball Beach track. The challenging sand, ocean views and sea air make it an exhilarating ride! Lightning McQueen decides to train outside in real conditions, rather than in the virtual reality of the simulator.

Have you heard?

When Cruz trains with Lightning at Fireball Beach, it's the first time she's ever coached a racer outside.

Who's the coach?

When Cruz tags along to Lightning's beach practice, she's the one who has problems. He has to teach her how to race on the sand and not get her tyres stuck.

Too much wheel spin

Sandy speedway

Fireball Beach was once one of the best races in the Piston Cup. The only downside was that when cars skidded around corners, fans in the stand were showered with sand!

Crazy contest

Lightning and Cruz accidentally find themselves competing in the demolition derby. They are totally unprepared for all the mayhem! Can they keep their cool and survive the Thunder Hollow Crazy Eight?

Explosions mark the start of the race.

Well-worn dirt track

Rough riders

The only things rougher than the Crazy Eight track are the racers. These bashed-up, smashed-up vehicles get bumped, bent, dented and nearly demolished – every single week!

THUNDER HOLLOW

Thunder Hollow Speedway is a rustic Piston Cup dirt track. But once a week, it transforms into the maddest demolition derby in America – the Crazy Eight! Competitors should expect crashed cars, crushed trucks and seriously dangerous driving!

Noisy, excited spectators

Figure of eight track shape

Have you heard?

Any vehicle can be a guest in the demolition derby. Doctor Damage blasts his ambulance sirens as he charges around the track!

Thunder Hollow Crazy Eight

The demolition derby racers rush around the figure eight speedway, ramming into each other until there is only one vehicle left. The last car standing is declared the winner!

Pile of plates

Miss Fritter loves to hang the license plates of her victims on her side. These trophies terrify the other cars, who wonder whether their plates will be next!

Horn-shaped smokestacks

True or False?

Miss Fritter is known as the Supreme Queen of Crashes.

FALSE: Her nickname is the Diva of Demolition.

Heavy chains to hold her hood down

Serious dents from years of smashing and crashing

MISS FRITTER

Miss Fritter is the fiercest and most feared competitor in the Thunder Hollow Crazy Eight demolition derby. Every week, the battered bus slams her rivals out of the race. She is determined to dent her way to victory!

License plate trophies

Fritter time

Anyone attending the demolition derby will hear Miss Fritter's army of rowdy fans. They love to chant, "It's Fritter Time!" whenever she is winning.

Fritter fears

Miss Fritter will give you the jitters! With her sharp, pointed smokestacks, and even sharper insults, she intimidates all who race against her.

Spinning, razor-sharp stop sign

MISS FRITTER

TOP SPEED:	As fast as is needed to scare rivals
OCCUPATION:	Professional demolition derby racer
VEHICLE TYPE:	Lower Belleville County Unified School District Bus

THOMASVILLE

Thomasville Speedway was Doc Hudson's home track, where the racing legend became famous. The top racers of the day once competed here. The speedway is now deserted and in disrepair, but there is still something special about it.

Lights and billboards still line the track.

Cruz speeding around the old track

Thomasville Speedway

A little inspiration

Thomasville may be run-down and ramshackle, but its powerful history fuels Lightning's imagination. Could a visit there help him focus on his training?

Have you heard?

There is a bar near the speedway called the Cotter Pin. Some retired racers still meet there.

Still standing

Thomasville was once a state-of-the-art stadium. It hasn't been used for many years, but the track is still intact and the grandstand is still standing.

Home of a legend

In its heyday, Thomasville was known as the home of the Fabulous Hudson Hornet. Fans would travel from far away just to get a glimpse of their hero in action!

THOMASVILLE SPEEDWAY ★★★
Home of 51 Fabulous Hudson Hornet

★ RACES EVERY WEEKEND! ★ FASTEST RACERS EVERY SUNDAY! ★

Grandstand and announcer box

Outbuildings and garages

The infield is overgrown with weeds.

Back on the track

When Lightning races on the old track, he feels like Doc is with him again. Connecting with his old mentor gives Lightning the inspiration he needs to keep on going.

SMOKEY

Smokey is famous in racing circles for discovering the Hudson Hornet. An amazing crew chief and mentor, Smokey turned a rookie into a true champion! These days, Smokey is retired from racing, but he has a lifetime of wisdom to pass on to others.

Legendary friends

Smokey hangs out with his racing buddies from the old days at the Cotte Pin. He is happy to take Lightning McQueen and Cruz to meet them.

1946 Hudson pickup truck

Brown paint finish

Smokey's garage logo

Smokey has a kind smile.

Outspoken Smokey

Straight-talking Smokey always speaks his mind. He may sound grumpy, but somewhere under that gruff exterior he has a softer, caring side.

"Funny what a racer can do when he's not overthinking things."
Smokey

Hometown hero

Smokey lives a quiet country life, but his garage is still in Thomasville, the place where he made his name. Smokey loves his hometown and has lived there for many years.

SMOKEY

TOP SPEED:	It's about wits, not speed
OCCUPATION:	Garage owner, semi-retired crew chief
VEHICLE TYPE:	1946 Hudson pickup truck
SPECIALTY:	Years of racing wisdom

Proud mentor

Smokey shows Lightning letters from Doc Hudson. They show how much Doc loved being McQueen's coach. This gives Lightning a new perspective on his old friend.

THE LEGENDS

In the 1950s, a generation of pioneering racers like the Hudson Hornet emerged, making it a magical time for the sport. Each of these Legends has some incredible stories to tell, and they are happy to share them with the track stars of today.

Have you heard?

Old rules of racing meant that Louise Nash had to steal her first number just to get on the track.

LOUISE NASH

RACE NUMBER: 94
ENGINE POWER: 125 HP
VEHICLE TYPE: 1950 Nash Ambassador

"Once we got on the track, we didn't want to leave."
Louise Nash

Two-tone paint is still immaculate.

Louise keeps herself in top condition.

Classic Whitewall tyres

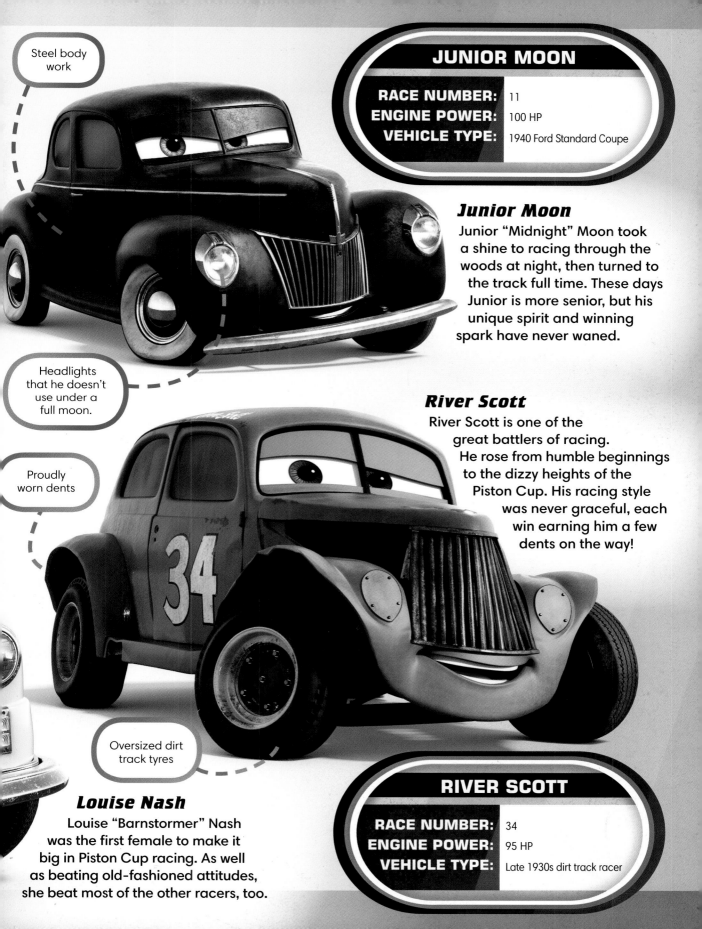

Steel body work

JUNIOR MOON

RACE NUMBER:	11
ENGINE POWER:	100 HP
VEHICLE TYPE:	1940 Ford Standard Coupe

Junior Moon

Junior "Midnight" Moon took a shine to racing through the woods at night, then turned to the track full time. These days Junior is more senior, but his unique spirit and winning spark have never waned.

Headlights that he doesn't use under a full moon.

River Scott

River Scott is one of the great battlers of racing. He rose from humble beginnings to the dizzy heights of the Piston Cup. His racing style was never graceful, each win earning him a few dents on the way!

Proudly worn dents

Oversized dirt track tyres

Louise Nash

Louise "Barnstormer" Nash was the first female to make it big in Piston Cup racing. As well as beating old-fashioned attitudes, she beat most of the other racers, too.

RIVER SCOTT

RACE NUMBER:	34
ENGINE POWER:	95 HP
VEHICLE TYPE:	Late 1930s dirt track racer

TRAINING WITH SMOKEY

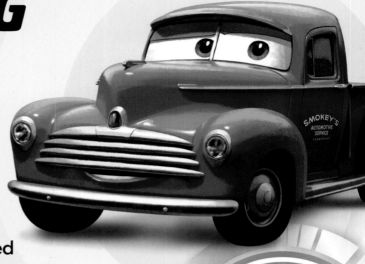

When Smokey comes out of retirement to coach Lightning McQueen, he uses old-school training methods tried and tested over the years. No simulators allowed! Can Doc Hudson's old crew chief return Lightning McQueen to his winning ways?

Jackson 2.0

With a little bodywork, Smokey makes Cruz look like Jackson Storm. Having a sparring partner helps Lightning to focus on beating his rival.

Wits to win

Smokey reminds Lightning about Doc Hudson's approach – if you can't outrun your rival, you have to outthink them. Speed isn't always the answer!

Moo manoeuvre

Smokey allows Lightning and Cruz to get caught right in the middle of a stampede of tractors! It's great practice for learning to manoeuvre around competitors.

Trailer training

Smokey makes Lightning pull a trailer, with the Legends onboard for extra weight! This helps Lightning to practice controlling torque instead of just using horsepower, and to avoid his wheels spinning.

Driving in the dark

Lightning must learn to trust his own instincts. Smokey believes that driving at night without any lights on is a great way for Lightning to get his confidence back.

Learning from Legends

Doc's old friends, the Legends, have years of racing experience. Cutting to the chase, their (very) direct advice guides and pushes Lightning to succeed!

Beach view
If you don't have tickets to the big race, you can still watch it on a large screen on the beach. The clever locals say that it's the perfect place to watch the Florida 500.

The stadium is packed for the Florida 500.

FLORIDA INTERNATIONAL SUPER SPEEDWAY

Ask racing fans what their favourite stadium is, and many will say the Florida International Super Speedway. The colossal size, awesome architecture and breathtaking beachside location delivers a carnival atmosphere to accompany the action on the track!

Florida 500

Each year, the Florida 500 is one of the Piston Cup's most eagerly awaited races. This year it's extra special – it's the opening race of the season and Lightning McQueen's unexpected comeback!

Pit Road

Exterior made from glass and aluminium

Boats watch from the harbour.

It's the pits

The stadium's trackside pit row is where the racers change tyres, stop for repairs or grab a drink! Each team of pitties must be lightning fast so that the racers get back out quickly.

53

FAST FRIENDS

Lightning and Cruz may have had a rocky start, but as they train and learn together, a mutual respect and great friendship forms. Cruz turns from fan to friend, while Lightning goes from trainee to trainer!

Crazy Eigh

Lightning and Cruz's craziest adventure is competing in the demolition derby Relying on each other to survive the race unscathed helps cement their friendship

Fireball Beach

At Fireball Beach, Lightning must show his trainer how to navigate through the sand. There's a lot that Cruz can learn from her so-called senior project!

Role reversal

It was Cruz's job to get Lightning back on the track. But as Lightning learns of Cruz's talent, he realises she could be an amazing racer. Perhaps it's her turn to shine, not his!

Ups and downs

All friendships have ups and downs. Cruz storms off when Lightning says she doesn't think like a racer. But the argument brings out the truth about her early dreams to race.

Star pupil

Along the way, Lightning begins to see Cruz's potential. By the time that he shows her some driving tricks, like drifting at Thomasville, he realises what a quick learner she is.

GO, CRUZ!

When Lightning McQueen realises that he can't win the Florida 500 race, he wonders whether Cruz could give it a better shot! He could coach and support her, just as Doc Hudson did for him. Could he give Cruz the guidance she needs for race success?

Lightning transforms from racer to crew chief.

Enter the mentor

When Lightning competes in the Florida 500, he has a lightbulb moment. He does a highly unusual move and insists that Cruz replaces him on the track halfway though the race. Her career is finally about to take off!

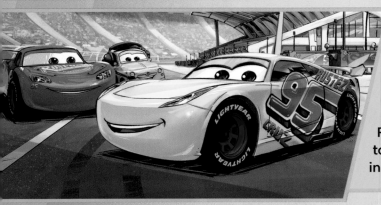

The new 95

To follow the race rules, Cruz must use the same number as Lightning. Luckily Ramone is on hand to paint a 95 on Cruz in record time.

Tractor trick

To help Cruz swerve past the other racers, Lightning reminds her of Smokey's training where she dodged a herd of tractors. His tip helps her move up the track.

Chasing the Storm

From his position at the front of the track, Jackson Storm takes no notice of Cruz. He doesn't see her as a threat – until she appears right on his tail, that is!

Fantastic flip!

Storm forces Cruz against a wall so she can't overtake him. Quick-thinking Cruz drives right up onto the wall and does an amazing flip in the air! She flies right over Storm – and across the finish line.

EXCLUSIVE INTERVIEW!

CRUZ AND LIGHTNING

PARTING WAYS

It is said that Rust-eze sponsor Mr. Sterling tried to hire his top trainer as his top racer, but Cruz turned him down. Ouch!

HI, PISTON CUP FANS!

Shannon Spokes here. Everybody's still talking about the historic joint win at the Florida 500. A few months later, I managed to catch up with the winners.

SPOKES: Well done on your victory at the Florida 500, guys! How did it feel?

RAMIREZ: It felt amazing! I dreamt of that moment for so long.

MCQUEEN: Helping Cruz felt just as good as any race I won myself. I'm back to winning – just not in the way I expected.

SPOKES: So you've signed with Dinoco rather than Rust-eze?

RAMIREZ: Yes, I'm proud to be part of the Dinoco family –

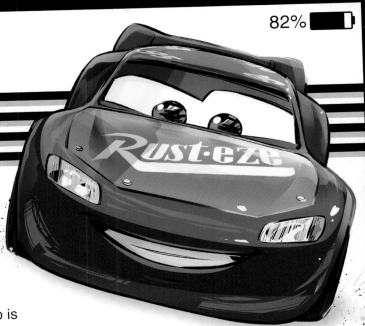

and even prouder to be wearing the number 51! It was once worn by the late, great Hudson Hornet.

SPOKES: The blue paint job is a big change, Lightning!

MCQUEEN: Like the new colour? It's the same as the one worn by my old mentor and inspiration, Doc Hudson.

SPOKES: The trackside gossip is that you're planning to retire from racing, Lightning. Any comment?

MCQUEEN: Who says I'm retiring? For now, I'm loving the new challenge of being Cruz's crew chief this season.

RAMIREZ: For now, we're on the same side, but perhaps we'll be racing rivals next season! Who knows?

SPOKES: So you guys are confident about winning this year's Piston Cup?

RAMIREZ: Obviously I'm still new to racing – I have a lot to learn! But I think that with a great mentor and friend like Mr. McQueen by my side, we have a pretty good shot.

MCQUEEN: We have a lot of work to do, but I think that with Cruz's skills and my experience, we can do anything.

⚡ MORE STORIES

GO TO RACER BIOS ›

Jackson Storm
Storm says that he's just as shocked as anyone else by the result.

Natalie Certain
Certain failed to predict the McQueen/Ramirez win. She had no data!

WHAT SORT OF RACER ARE YOU?

If you are considering a career on the track, it helps to know which type of racer you are. Are you a high-tech Next Gen? Perhaps you're more like one of the classic racing legends? Or is the demolition derby more your can of oil? Take this quiz to find out!

Answer the following five questions, choosing A, B or C.

 It's time for a practice session. Which method do you choose?

1

A) An intense session on the simulator, to see if you can improve your lap time.

B) A challenging spin on your local out-of-town dirt track.

C) Smash and crash into a few rocks, walls, cacti – anything in the way, really.

 What motivates you to win each race

2

A) Proving to everyone that you're the fastest racer on the track. You need to be the one in the spotlight!

B) Winning the Piston Cup for all your fans and friends back home.

C) Seeing your dented opponent do a triple flip into a ditch.

3 Your trusted transporter is getting a makeover and asks for your advice. What do you say?

A) Make sure your colours match mine exactly. We must project the right image!

B) It's up to you. Whatever looks cool and makes you feel comfortable.

C) Transporter? I don't need no transporter! I only race at the county track!

4 It's the closing laps of a race, but you're still behind the winner. What tactics you deploy?

A) Increase my speed by 0.7%, while reducing my angle around the corner by 0.2%. This ensures consistent weight distribution.

B) Summon extra energy, then find the perfect moment to edge past the leader on the last corner.

C) Simple. Ram him off the road! BOOM!

5 Which of the following nicknames do you prefer?

A) The Supreme Machine
B) The Chilled Champion
C) The Dentmeister

Answers

Mainly As:
You're a Next Gen like Jackson Storm. It's all about technology and data. That's what helps you win!

Mainly Bs:
You're a classic racer like Lightning McQueen. Passion and tactics are what makes you a champion.

Mainly Cs:
You're a demolition derby contestant like Miss Fritter. You'd rather be smashing than dashing!

ACKNOWLEDGEMENTS

Penguin
Random
House

Senior Art Editor Lynne Moulding
Editor Lauren Nesworthy
Designers Lisa Rogers, Abi Wright
Pre-production Producer Marc Staples
Producer Zara Markland
Managing Editor Sadie Smith
Managing Art Editor Ron Stobbart
Publisher Julie Ferris
Art Director Lisa Lanzarini
Publishing Director Simon Beecroft

First published in Great Britain in 2017 by
Dorling Kindersley Limited
80 Strand, London WC2R 0RL
A Penguin Random House Company

10 9 8 7 6 5 4 3 2 1
001–299056–May/2017